Dips, Salsas & Spreads

Dips, Salsas & Spreads

Text by Judith Dunham
and Jane Horn

CollinsPublishersSanFrancisco
A Division of HarperCollins*Publishers*

First published in USA 1996 by Collins Publishers San Francisco
1160 Battery Street, San Francisco, CA 94111-1213
HarperCollins Web Site: http://www.harpercollins.com

Produced by Weldon Owen Inc.

Associate Publisher: Anne Dickerson
Managing Editor: Judith Dunham
Editorial Assistant: Hannah Rahill
Text Authors: Judith Dunham, Jane Horn
Copy Editors: Sharon Silva, Judith Dunham
Proofreaders: Sharilyn Hovind, Desne Border
Index: Ken Dellapenta
Design Concept: John Bull
Design: Kari Perin, Perin + Perin
Collins Publishers San Francisco
Series Editor: Meesha Halm
Production: Lynne Noone, Susan Swant, Kristen Wurz

Library of Congress Cataloging-in-Publication Data
Horn, Jane 1945–
Dips, salsas & spreads / text by Jane Horn: edited by Judith Dunham.
p.   cm. — (Easy entertaining series)
At head of title: Featuring recipes from the best-selling Beautiful Cookbook series.
Includes index.
ISBN 0-00-225043-8
1. Dips (Appetizers) 2. Salsas (Cookery) 3. Entertaining.
I. Dunham, Judith. II. Title. III. Series.
TX740.H643   1996
641.8' 12—dc20   95-47666

Manufactured by Toppan
Printed in China
3 5 7 9 10 8 6 4

Front cover: left to right: Tapénade, Salt Cod Mousse
Back cover: clockwise from top: Tomatillo Salsa, Pineapple Salsa, Pumpkin Seed Salsa
Title page: top to bottom: Pinto Bean Dip and Roasted Red Bell Pepper Dip garnished with crudités and tortilla chips.

CONTENTS

INTRODUCTION

A gathering of friends who enjoy one another's company is an interlude that slows the passage of time. It is an island apart from the sea of hectic activities and obligations. Yet it's often hard to fit entertaining into a busy schedule. This book offers a solution: there isn't a quicker menu to prepare for company than a serve-yourself banquet of appetizers, and the easiest to prepare are dips, salsas and spreads. Dips are generally thin mixtures, such as a creamy bean or eggplant purée, that will easily coat a tortilla chip, fruit slice or skewered vegetable. Spreads are commonly thicker—herbed cheese or roasted garlic—and require a knife for smoothing atop a cracker, vegetable round or pita triangle. Salsas, dips and spreads, matched with vegetables, fruits and breads, let a party run itself.

Not only are dips, salsas and spreads fast to prepare, but many of them can (and should) be made ahead of time. When these dishes are set aside for a day or just an hour, their flavors intermingle, ripen and intensify. Before moving to center stage, they need only the lightest of finishing touches: one last stir, a slice of lime, a sprinkling of chives. Other recipes can be assembled well in advance and then, as you pour the first glasses of wine for guests, made into a delectable whole.

An entire chapter in this book honors the status of salsa, one of the most popular condiments today. Reliable favorites—chunky mixtures of hot chilies, fresh tomatoes, tart tomatillos, creamy avocados—are joined by welcome innovations that sweeten the fire of chilies with papaya, mango or pineapple. The spreads and dips take your entertaining to other regions of the world. Emerging with ease from the food processor are

sophisticated starters like warm, pungent Eggplant Caviar and savory Tapénade, thick with olives. You can venture into the versatile dips and choose luscious purées laced with herbs or aromatic sauces redolent of anchovies. When unexpected guests arrive with a bottle of wine in hand, reach for your favorite olive oil and assemble a platter of vegetables for dipping, and your party has officially started.

These recipes allow you to cater to your guests' nutritional preferences. Well over half of the dishes are vegetarian (noted for instant reference with the 🅥 symbol). And many are free of dairy products. There are plenty of tasty options for reduced-fat appetizers, too. No wonder that salsas—low in fat, rich in vegetables and fruits—are always a hit.

Preparing dips, salsas and spreads sparks creativity and brings out the artist in everyone. Partner your salsa with slices of jicama or fingers of green, red and yellow bell pepper. Place them next to baskets of plain and salted tortilla chips. Offer platters of halved baby zucchini and sliced fennel as sturdy mates for

spreads, alongside squares of toasted dark bread. An infinitely wide palette of vegetables and fruits in season—florets of cauliflower and broccoli, tomatoes red, yellow or green, apples and pears in bright and subtle hues—can be set out for guests to dunk into a salsa, stir into a dip or carry a spread.

Other sections of this book contain tips to help you develop a strategy for entertaining. You'll discover the key to maintaining a well-stocked pantry. You'll learn how to choose serving ware and accessories and present your appetizers with style. Menu suggestions help you combine your favorite dips, salsas and spreads into an hors d'oeuvre party and expand them into a complete meal. Whether you're anticipating a party that's weeks away or inviting colleagues to your home at the end of the workday, you'll be prepared.

When you have a strategy for entertaining, your confidence is boosted, and you can reclaim time. Your sense of relaxation will permeate your party. You are free to join the ebb and flow of conversations. You can even raise a glass and toast yourself.

THE WELL-STOCKED PANTRY

Is your pantry is a spacious, shelf-lined alcove? Or is your kitchen storage confined to a couple of cabinets? Either way, it can be your best helper when you entertain with the recipes in this book. The most important ingredients in a practical pantry are planning and organization. Start to plan your pantry by analyzing your style of entertaining. If you invite company infrequently but in large numbers, for instance, you will want to store ingredients in quantity so you can prepare a single party from the pantry, then restock before your next event. Whether you customarily entertain casual gatherings or host more formal events will influence the kinds of dishes you make and the quantities of foods you need on hand.

With your approach to entertaining in mind, you're ready to create menus, like those suggested on pages 20–23, using the recipes in this book. Their ingredients become the foundation for your pantry. Among these ingredients are fresh fruits, vegetables and herbs that can be purchased a day or more in advance of your party. Also included are versatile foods that can be plucked from the pantry for spur-of-the-moment entertaining. As you customize your pantry, remember to take advantage of proven shortcuts. You may prefer the flavor of freshly roasted peppers, tomatoes in season, home-cooked beans and just-squeezed lemon and lime juices. However, good-quality prepared and prepackaged versions of these indispensable ingredients can be stored in your pantry or refrigerator and used in dips and spreads without sacrificing taste.

The final step is to organize the contents of your pantry. Frequently used items such as olive oil, crackers and herbs and spices should be accessible. Cases of wine or mineral water and extra canned goods do not need to take up valuable space in the kitchen and could be stored in another location. Refrigerated foods that you will need at preparation time should be grouped on the same shelf or in the same bin.

Note the date of purchase for spices and dried herbs and for other foods that lose flavor or freshness after long storage. Grains, nuts, beans and other foods purchased in bulk need to be transferred to airtight containers and labeled before storing. You may want to post inside your pantry cabinet a list of ingredients. Simply mark the items that need to be replaced before your next party.

OLIVE OIL

For preparing the recipes in this book, you will want to choose a premium olive oil. Extra-virgin olive oil, the highest quality of the various grades on the market, has a distinctive fruity aroma, a full-bodied flavor and a clear, deep green color. Because the olives for this grade are processed without the use of heat, extra-virgin olive oils are also labeled cold-pressed. Olive oils are classified on the basis of their acidity. Extra-virgin has the lowest acid content. Virgin olive oil and pure olive oil are somewhat higher in acidity and are more suitable for using in cooking rather than uncooked dishes.

Equally versatile for entertaining are flavored olive oils. Infused with the taste, aroma and color of herbs, garlic, mushrooms, sun-dried tomatoes or chilies, for example, these oils can be used to season cooked and uncooked foods. Vegetables can be coated with herb-infused oil before they are laid on the grill, or a dip or spread can be garnished with a drizzling of oil in a complementary flavor. For truly fast and easy entertaining, set out flavored olive oils next to extra-virgin olive oil as dips for vegetables and breads.

Storage: Olive oil will keep up to 6 months stored in a cool, dark place. Flavored olive oil containing fresh ingredients should be refrigerated.

VINEGAR

A selection of vinegars in your pantry expands your entertaining options. A vinaigrette that combines your favorite oil and vinegar makes an instant dip for raw vegetables or a quick marinade for blanched vegetables. A sprinkling of wine or flavored vinegar serves as a piquant topping for a purée or spread. Lettuce, arugula or other greens sprinkled with vinegar form a deliciously edible bed for a salsa.

In addition to such staples as red and white wine vinegar and apple cider vinegar, you'll want to stock, and experiment with, balsamic vinegar, flavored vinegars, sherry vinegar and champagne vinegar. Balsamic vinegar, an aged, deep reddish brown vinegar that is a specialty of Modena, Italy, has a piquant sweet-and-sour taste. Flavored vinegars are white wine vinegars that have been infused with herbs—basil, tarragon, oregano—or steeped with chilies, garlic or fruit such as raspberries.

Storage: Vinegars will keep up to 6 months stored in a cool, dark place.

OLIVES AND CAPERS

Not only are olives an essential ingredient in such classic Mediterranean spreads as Caponata (page 90) and Tapénade (page 82), but a banquet of various imported olives in a handsome serving bowl couldn't be quicker to assemble for company.

Used whole, halved or sliced, olives also make a zesty garnish for many spreads and dips. Both green (unripe) and black (ripe) olives are cured in salt, garlic, brine, vinegar and oil to give them flavors ranging from mild and mellow to pungent and spicy. Green olives are available pitted and stuffed with pimiento, anchovies, capers, garlic or almonds. The French Niçoise and the Greek Kalamata—varieties of black olives cured in brine—are only two of the many you may want to have on hand. Consider the Italian Gaeta, cured in salt, and dry-cured black olives with their wrinkly skins. Or enliven bland commercial black olives by layering them with garlic; oregano, thyme, bay or other herbs; chilies; and orange or lemon zest. Add extra-virgin olive oil and wine vinegar and refrigerate for at least 5 days before serving.

Capers are the small, round buds of a bush native to the Mediterranean region. Ranging from the size of a peppercorn to the size of a pea, they are pickled in vinegar or packed in salt (rinse lightly before use) and added to dishes as an ingredient or employed as a garnish. For the finest flavor, look for imported capers.

Storage: Unopened canned or bottled olives can be stored in a cool, dark place for up to 6 months. These olives, once opened, and those purchased in bulk should be stored in a nonmetallic container in the refrigerator, where they may be kept 2–3 weeks. Bottled capers will keep several months in the refrigerator; salted capers for several months at room temperature.

ANCHOVIES AND TUNA

Anchovies impart a distinctive savory flavor and a welcome hint of saltiness to both cooked and uncooked preparations. They are most commonly marketed as fillets, packed flat in oil in cans. Look for brands specifying the use of olive oil. Whole anchovies preserved in salt are sold in large cans or by the pound in some delicatessens; the fish must be filleted and lightly rinsed before use. The fillets are also puréed into a paste available in tubes (substitute 1 teaspoon paste for each anchovy fillet). Canned pink-flecked tuna in olive oil has a rich flavor that can't be duplicated by tuna packed in water. Seek out an Italian brand for the finest results.

Storage: Canned anchovies and tuna, unopened, can be stored for 1 year at room temperature. Once opened, they can be refrigerated for 1–2 days. Anchovy paste, once opened, can be kept 6 months in the refrigerator.

NUTS

Almonds, pine nuts and walnuts add flavor and texture to a host of spreads and dips in this book. You may want to tuck away a variety of other nuts for garnishes and party snacks. Whole cashews, macadamias and Brazils, as well as roasted and salted, smoked or flavored almonds, pistachios and other nuts, are easy to pull from the pantry and set out for company. Toasting shelled nuts (page 17) before serving them or using them in recipes enhances their flavor and can be done in advance.

Storage: Shelled nuts should be kept in an airtight container in a cool, dark place or in the refrigerator. They should be used within 6 months.

BEANS AND PEAS

As abundantly shown by the recipes in this book, beans and peas can be cooked and puréed with a variety of ingredients and flavorings to make distinctive spreads and dips. In many other ways, they are a boon for easy entertaining. Recipes with beans and peas can often be made a day or so ahead of a party

and often taste better when flavors have had a chance to meld. Or beans can be cooked and refrigerated 1 or 2 days in advance of assembling a recipe calling for them. In a pinch, canned beans can be substituted in most recipes. Remember to drain well and rinse before serving. Stock a variety of beans, including black beans, chick-peas, fava beans, Great Northern beans, refried beans and different types of lentils.

Storage: Keep dried beans in an airtight container in a cool, dark place up to 1 year. Canned beans, unopened, can be stored indefinitely. Once opened, they should be refrigerated in an airtight container and used within 2 or 3 days.

VEGETABLES

Without question, vegetables are the linchpin of easy entertaining. For nearly all dips, spreads and salsas, vegetables—raw or marinated, blanched or roasted—are among the first choice for accompaniments. Seasonality must be considered when selecting vegetables. Experiment by accompanying recipes in this book with whatever locally grown fresh vegetables are available.

Varieties of sun-dried tomatoes and dried mushrooms, included in the pantry, can be reconstituted if you need to make a quick substitution for the fresh product in some recipes. Sun-dried tomatoes, roasted peppers, artichoke hearts or mushrooms packed in olive oil can be drained and served alongside a cheese spread and a basket of crackers.

Storage: Fresh vegetables such as greens and mushrooms need to be used within 2 or 3 days after purchase. Hardier vegetables such as carrots, celery, radishes and zucchini will keep 1 week in the refrigerator. Dried vegetables, stored in an airtight container at room temperature, will keep 6 months.

FRUITS

Apple and pear slices provide a sweet and refreshing counterpoint to a platter featuring a cheese spread or vegetable dip and pita bread chips or crackers. Fresh fruits in season—berries, grapes, pineapple chunks, papaya spears, melon wedges, kiwifruit slices—can be arranged on an attractive tray, garnished with fresh mint and presented as an hors d'oeuvre.

Dried fruits such as apples, apricots and figs are handy pantry staples that can be set on a serving plate with a selection of nuts for instant party food. Bottled lemon and lime juices should be kept in stock in case you unexpectedly run out of the fresh fruit. Lemon juice has an indispensable use when preparing fresh produce for company: sliced vegetables and fruits sprinkled with lemon juice or dipped in a bath of 1 part juice and 4 parts water will not turn brown.

Storage: Keep most ripe fruits in the refrigerator; to improve their flavor, allow them to come to room temperature before serving. Citrus fruits will keep in the refrigerator 3–4 weeks, other fruits for about 1 week. Stored in an airtight container in the refrigerator, dried fruits will keep up to 1 year.

HERBS AND SPICES

If you are fortunate enough to have a windowsill or backyard herb garden, you can readily pick fresh herbs—such as parsley, dill, mint, basil, chives, rosemary, thyme, bay leaves and chervil—for seasonings or to use as garnishes. Many of these fresh herbs are usually sold as bundled sprigs in the fresh vegetable section of well-stocked supermarkets. Dried herbs in the pantry ensure that you'll always have seasonings on hand. You'll also want to stock peppercorns, both black and white,

and the ground spices used in the recipes in this book, including allspice, cayenne pepper, cumin, dried chili and turmeric, and blends such as curry powder and Cajun-style seasoning.

Storage: Fresh herbs should be wrapped in a damp paper towel and stored in the refrigerator, where they will last up to 1 week. Dried herbs and spices should be marked with the date of purchase, stored in airtight containers in a cool, dark place and replaced, if not used, within 1 year.

BREADS AND CRACKERS

Modifying the cliché, you could describe bread and its relatives as the staff of entertaining. A basketful of sliced, fresh bread—whole wheat, sourdough, herb, seeded—alone is a feast for company. Breads such as focaccia or quick breads made with fruits and vegetables are substantial enough to serve on their own, without an accompaniment. Bread sticks, tortilla chips, lavash crackers, mini bagels and pita bread all complement a wide array of salsas, dips and spreads. If you have a loaf of bread that is 2 or 3 days old, you can turn it into bread crumbs or croutons (page 16) and add them to the pantry.

Storage: Fresh bread, stored in a plastic bag, will keep 1–2 days in a cool, dark place. Crackers should be stored in an airtight container in a cool, dark place and used within 3 months.

BEVERAGES

No other category of entertaining staple is easier to store than a selection of wines, spirits, mineral waters, beers, sodas and other beverages. If you host large groups or entertain frequently, and have the space to spare, you can purchase cases of beverages. Most beverages in bottles and cans will keep indefinitely.

SPECIALTY INGREDIENTS

Many of the following foods from the recipes in this book are available in well-stocked supermarkets and can also be found in markets devoted to foods of a particular region. If you regularly serve Thai dishes for guests or if Mediterranean cuisine is a frequent choice for your entertaining, plan a trip to a specialty market to stock up on these pantry items in quantity.

ASIAN AND INDIAN FOODS

Dried shrimp: Small or large, peeled sun-dried shrimp impart a pungent taste to savory dips and spreads. Sold in small plastic bags or in bulk, they can be stored indefinitely in an airtight container at room temperature.

Fish sauce (nam pla): Made from fermented anchovies, this Thai sauce is a thin, salty liquid with strong flavor. Sold in bottles, it can be stored indefinitely at room temperature.

Garam masala: This aromatic Indian blend of dried ground spices, which differ depending on the place of origin, may include cardamom, cloves, cinnamon, fennel, coriander, cumin and turmeric. Marketed in small cans or jars, *garam masala* should be stored in an airtight container. Commercial curry powder may be substituted.

Ghee: This Indian version of clarified butter—butter from which the milk solids have been removed—does not burn when used at high temperatures. Sold in bottles, plastic containers or cans, it should be refrigerated and will keep for 3–4 weeks. To make your own clarified butter, see page 17.

Green Thai chili (prik khee noo): Essential to Thai cooking, this small fresh chili is very hot. Start with a little and add more to taste. Red chilies, also available, are less fiery.

Palm sugar (nam taan peep): This Thai sweetener is available in dry cubes and as a thick paste. It should be stored in an airtight container at room temperature.

Seasoned rice vinegar: White or pale colored, this mild-flavored Japanese vinegar is sold in bottles that can be stored in the pantry alongside other vinegars.

Shrimp paste (gapi): A strong-tasting Thai seasoning made from fermented, salted shrimp, this fine purée is sold in jars. It should be stored in an airtight container as its smell can overpower other spices and seasonings.

LATIN FOODS

Chilies: A staple of Mexican and American Southwestern cooking, chilies come fresh and dried in varieties that differ in color, flavor and heat. Fresh chilies include the Anaheim, jalapeño, poblano, serrano and habanero; dried, the ancho, chipotle and pasilla. Preserved chilies are available in cans and bottles.

Green pumpkin seeds (pepitas): The seeds from the heart of the pumpkin are most commonly sold hulled.

Ground dried red chili: Unlike most commercial chili powders that are a blend of dried ground chilies combined with other seasonings, pure chili powder is made solely from ground dried chilies and is much hotter.

Manchego cheese: This cheese has a rich and mellow flavor. Monterey jack may be substituted.

Nopalitos: The fleshy oval pads or leaves of the cactus plant, diced or sliced, are available canned or pickled.

Refried beans: Beans that have been cooked, then mashed and fried in lard, are sold in cans. Nonfat versions of refried beans, which are vegetarian, are also available.

Tomatillos: Small, tart and lemony, tomatillos look like green tomatoes in a brown husk. They are available fresh and canned.

MEDITERRANEAN AND MIDDLE EASTERN FOODS

Mullet roe (tarama): Imported from Greece, mullet roe is packed in salt or oil and sold in jars.

Pomegranate juice and syrup: The ruby-colored tart-sweet juice extracted from pomegranate fruit is available in bottles. The syrup is a bottled concentrate made from pomegranate juice. It can be diluted to make pomegranate juice by adding 1 cup of water to $1^{1}/_{2}$ tablespoons syrup. Store opened bottles in the refrigerator.

Tahini: This thick, oily paste of ground sesame seeds is sold in bottles and cans. Tahini separates on standing and should be stirred before using to reincorporate the oil that rises to the top. Stored in the refrigerator, it keeps 3–4 months.

PANTRY TECHNIQUES

These basic techniques appear throughout the book or offer homemade alternatives to purchased ingredients. Bread crumbs, clarified butter, croutons, peeled and seeded tomatoes, pita bread chips, tortilla chips, roasted peppers and toasted nuts and seeds can be prepared and stored as part of your pantry until needed.

HANDLING CHILIES

Chilies, especially fresh chilies, must be handled with care, as they contain capsaicin, which can irritate the skin. Most of the heat in a chili comes from the capsaicin in the ribs and seeds, only 10 percent from the flesh. Wear rubber gloves when working with chilies and be careful not to rub your eyes or face. As soon as you have finished working with the chilies, wash your hands and any utensils you have used with warm soapy water.

MAKING BREAD CRUMBS

What's left of a loaf of bread that is less than fresh, but still flavorful, can be turned into fresh or dried bread crumbs. For fresh bread crumbs: Slice the bread and trim the crusts, if desired. Process in a food processor fitted with the metal blade or in a blender, or place on a cutting surface and flake with a fork. For dried bread crumbs: Arrange fresh crumbs on a baking sheet and place in a 325°F oven until dry, 15–20 minutes. One slice of bread yields about $^3/_4$ cup fresh crumbs or about $^1/_4$ cup dried crumbs. Crumbs can be stored in an airtight heavy-duty plastic bag in the freezer.

MAKING CROUTONS

Day-old bread, plain or flavored, can be recycled into croutons. Cut the bread into slices about $^1/_2$ inch thick, or as thick or thin as you like (smaller cubes toast faster; larger cubes take longer to dry out). Stack the slices and cut lengthwise into strips $^1/_2$ inch wide, then cut crosswise to create cubes that are $^1/_2$ inch square. Place the cubes in a bowl, toss with a little extra-virgin olive oil and season to taste with salt and pepper. Transfer to a baking sheet and bake in a 350°F oven, tossing occasionally, until golden brown and crisp, 15–20 minutes.

MAKING PITA BREAD CHIPS

When baked, wedges of pita bread become more crisp and flavorful without any added fat. Cut large pita rounds, regular or whole wheat, into 8 wedges. Set on a baking sheet and place in a 375°F oven. Toast until lightly browned and crisp, about 5 minutes (the chips will dry out further as they cool). Store in an airtight container at room temperature for about 3 days.

MAKING TORTILLA CHIPS

When you make your own tortilla chips, they taste fresher, and you can control the salt and other seasonings. Cut each corn tortilla into 6 wedges. Pour corn or vegetable oil into a deep, heavy frying pan to a depth of $1^1/_2$–2 inches and heat to 360°F, or until a small piece of tortilla starts to brown within moments of being dropped in the oil. Working in batches, add the tortilla wedges and fry until crisp and golden, 30–60 seconds. Using a slotted spoon, transfer the chips to paper towels to drain. Sprinkle with salt, if desired, and store in an airtight container at room temperature for 2–3 days.

PEELING AND SEEDING TOMATOES

To peel a fresh tomato, cut a shallow X in the blossom end with a paring knife. Fill a saucepan with water, place over high heat and bring to a boil. Drop the tomato into the boiling water for about 15 seconds, then plunge it into a bowl of cold water. Cut out the stem end and pull off the skin. To seed a tomato, cut it in half and gently squeeze out the seeds and juices. Use a finger or a small knife to scrape away any remaining seeds. Store the tomatoes in an airtight container in the refrigerator for 3–4 days.

PREPARING CLARIFIED BUTTER

In a small saucepan over low heat, melt 1 cup unsalted butter without stirring. Skim any white foam from the surface and discard, then slowly pour the clear liquid into a container. Discard the milky residue in the bottom of the pan. Clarified butter stored in an airtight container will keep 3–4 weeks in the refrigerator, several weeks longer in the freezer.

ROASTING BELL PEPPERS AND CHILIES

Many recipes call for roasting bell peppers and chilies in order to remove their skins and to heighten their flavors. Arrange peppers or chilies on a baking sheet and slip under a preheated broiler, place them on a grill rack over a charcoal fire or spear them, one at a time, on a fork and hold over an open flame.

Turn the peppers or chilies as needed to blacken and blister the skins evenly on all sides. Remove from the heat and enclose in a paper or plastic bag or cover with a kitchen towel until cool enough to handle, about 10 minutes. Using your fingers or a small knife, peel off the blackened skin. Remove the stem and seeds and cut as directed in individual recipes. Peeled, roasted peppers can be stored in an airtight container in the refrigerator for up to 3 days.

TOASTING AND GRINDING NUTS AND SEEDS

Toasting pine nuts, walnuts, almonds and seeds such as pumpkin or sesame boosts their flavor, deepens their color and increases their crunchiness. Place the nuts or seeds in a heavy, dry frying pan over medium-low heat. Stir and toss gently until lightly browned and fragrant (pine nuts burn easily, so watch them closely). Alternatively, place the nuts or seeds on a baking sheet in a 350°F oven and toast, stirring occasionally, until browned and fragrant, 8–10 minutes. Nuts and seeds can be ground in a nut mill. They can also be ground in a food processor fitted with the metal blade or in a blender; do not overprocess or they will release their oils and turn into a paste.

THE ART OF PRESENTATION

A menu of salsas, dips and spreads, by definition, guarantees that guests will serve themselves. Once you've set out food for company, only a few tasks—replenishing the bread basket or opening another bottle of wine—will momentarily draw you back into the kitchen. How could hosting a party be easier? As well as helping a party flow smoothly, a modicum of attention to presentation makes each recipe in this book, no matter how simple, look delectable and enticing and a display of several dishes lavish and harmonious.

A practical way to begin formulating your party logistics is to survey the serving dishes you already have in your kitchen. Earmark which are best for particular recipes and which have a convenient versatility: small and medium bowls for spreads, salsas and dips; platters of various sizes for fruit and vegetable accompaniments; baskets for breads and crackers; an array of dishes for nibbles such as olives and nuts. For quick access when you need them, store these pieces in handy locations.

If you think you might run short of serving pieces, you can borrow plates and bowls from a set of dinnerware. Don't worry if the diversity looks like a hodgepodge. Instead, take advantage of different colors and patterns by creatively playing them off against one another and the foods in your menu. A brilliantly colored, geometrically shaped bowl can enhance a subtly hued spread. A clear glass bowl opens a window onto the rainbow colors of a homemade salsa. Your collection can also be expanded—and your inventiveness complimented by

your guests—when you hollow out a loaf of bread or a vegetable or fruit, such as a bell pepper, melon, head of cabbage or radicchio, or beefsteak tomato—to enlist as a container.

Whether your final goal is a table that looks sparely elegant or joyously festive, you can have fun layering colors and textures. A bed of greens on a serving platter forms a canvas for a composition of variously shaped and colored vegetables and fruits. A napkin, even of white damask, nestled in a basket not only cushions a bread-and-cracker assortment, but also enlivens a pairing that might otherwise look a bit bland. Herb sprigs, a few edible flowers, lemon and lime wedges, a sprinkling of capers or a drizzling of flavored olive oil from your pantry—these and other ingredients can be readied in advance and set aside for garnishing the dishes at the last minute. Remember that such aesthetic details, minor though they may seem, multiply to create a grand effect.

Setup tasks, which are time-consuming when left to the hours just before guests arrive, can largely be done in the morning or the previous day. As soon as you decide where you want to lay out the food, choose tablecloths or place mats and arrange them. Then lay out serving utensils and napkins, and small hors d'oeuvre plates and sets of knives and forks if your menu calls for them. To make the knives and forks look attractive, gang them in a napkin-lined basket rather than pile them loosely on the table. Since this is a serve-yourself party, you may want to pick a table or countertop to be used exclusively

for beverages, so guests can freely help themselves. Beverages that don't require refrigeration can be assembled there in advance along with glasses and small napkins.

If you have even a day or two to prepare for your party, walk through the entire setup in your imagination to glean any time-savers you can do ahead, making a list if you'd find it helpful. Do candles in holders need replacing, ice-cube trays refilling,

cloth napkins folding? No task is too insignificant to fit into a spare moment. Perhaps you'll need a tray to carry small serving bowls of dips to the table or a pitcher to hold a cold beverage. Take these items out of their cabinets. Every trip or two you save walking back and forth across the kitchen will add to the pleasure you'll have at the main event.

MENUS

An Impromptu Get-Together

SERVES 6

With a well-stocked pantry, spontaneous entertaining is both possible and a pleasure. For this menu, shortcuts are the key. A food processor or blender is a must to make instant purées. Buy pitted olives and blend together a rich Tapénade in minutes. Use canned chick-peas for an equally fast, delicious Hummus spread. The Tuna Pâté also assembles in minutes. Ready-cut raw vegetables, sold packaged at most supermarkets, can serve as dippers for the oil. Willow baskets, rustic pottery serving bowls and platters, and textured checkered napkins create an appealing ambiance for these foods from the countryside.

Hummus with carrot sticks, lavash crackers
and bread sticks

Tapénade with endive leaves and crusty French bread
or baguette slices

Tuna Pâté with crackers or pita bread chips

Vegetables Dipped in Oil using celery stalks,
carrot sticks, cherry tomatoes, red and yellow bell pepper
slices, steamed snow peas and broccoli florets

Late-Night Snack

SERVES 4

After an evening at the movies or the theater, invite friends to enjoy a menu of après-performance treats that can be made a day ahead and refrigerated. Add sparks to the gathering by serving two dipping sauces—one spiced with Thai chilies, the other enlivened with Thai fish sauce. With plentiful supplies of Asian ingredients in your pantry, you won't have to venture out for last-minute shopping. Roasted Red Bell Pepper Dip, with its hint of cumin and its warm hue, complements the dips from Southeast Asia. The heat of the food may need cooling with beer and iced tea.

Spicy Shrimp Sauce with green onions,
sliced cucumbers and blanched baby carrots

Thai Dipping Sauce with grilled skewered prawns
and steamed baby bok choy leaves

Roasted Red Bell Pepper Dip with toast triangles

Antipasti Alfresco

SERVES 8

You need go only as far as your backyard, terrace or deck to treat guests to an idyllic outdoor gathering. Everything can be assembled hours ahead. For a party this size, you'll want to double the recipes for Charred Onion and Garlic Spread and Roasted Red Bell Pepper Dip. Make the topping for the rounds of Brie in advance; when guests start arriving, just slip the cheese into the oven. Offer chilled mineral waters and sodas from an ice-filled tub and a fruity Chardonnay.

Brie with Roasted Garlic and Olives with
apple wedges and toasted baguette slices

Charred Onion and Garlic Spread
with crackers and bread sticks

Roasted Red Bell Pepper Dip with steamed
asparagus spears and cauliflower and broccoli florets

Sesame-Eggplant Purée with pita bread chips or
flat bread, or slathered on wedges of focaccia

A Provençal Lunch

SERVES 6–8

Pretend your dining room is a café in Avignon or an intimate restaurant in Nice. Alongside this light lunch showcasing the tastes of Provence, serve spiced olives (page 10) and roasted bell peppers (page 17) sliced thinly lengthwise and drizzled with a simple vinaigrette of extra-virgin olive oil and balsamic vinegar. Although you can halve the recipe for Ratatouille to serve 6–8, you can just as easily make the full amount and savor the extra the following day. For each guest at the party, fold a cotton napkin decorated with a Provençal print around a fork and knife. Set out bottles of mineral water and a pitcher of iced herbal tea with plenty of lemon wedges.

Aïoli with a platter of green onions, sliced fennel,
baby carrots and blanched green beans

Anchovy Spread with Garlic

Salt Cod Mousse on slices of French bread

Ratatouille garnished with chopped fresh basil
and spooned on seeded crackers

After-School Party

SERVES 8

At the end of the school day, entertain your children and their friends with a Mexican-inspired treat. To serve 8, double each recipe. If you involve the children in the minimal preparation, the fun starts before they feast on this nutritious menu. With your guidance, they can chop the tomatoes, mash the avocados, mix the Guacamole and stir the bean dip. The amount of chilies in the salsa may be adjusted to suit their taste. Instead of a chafing dish for the Pinto Bean Dip, use a microwave-safe bowl and gently reheat the dip as necessary. Gathered around the kitchen table to enjoy this south-of-the-border snack, the children can balance cheerfully colored paper napkins to catch the drips and crumbs, and quench their thirst with a selection of cold fruit juices.

Guacamole with celery stalks and carrot sticks

Pinto Bean Dip with heated flour and corn tortillas

Tomato Salsa with tortilla chips and corn chips

Salsa Fiesta

SERVES 6–8

On a summer weekend evening, salsas can star as an hors d'oeuvre assortment, then expand the party into a meal when served as condiments for grilled chicken, fish and shellfish. Use brightly colored bowls and linens and assemble a festive centerpiece. Serve margaritas and tequila sunrises in thick blue Mexican glasses. For a memorable drink, make your own pepper vodka: Steep fiery chiltepín or other chilies in a 4-cup bottle of vodka for up to 10 days. When the vodka is as hot as you like, strain through a fine sieve and rebottle. Serve well chilled, over ice or mixed into Bloody Marys.

Charred Green Salsa with blue-corn tortilla chips

Roasted Vegetable Salsa with baked pita bread chips
or spooned on baguette slices brushed
with garlic and extra-virgin olive oil and grilled

Pumpkin Seed Salsa with mini cheese quesadillas,
nachos or tortilla chips

Papaya-Pepper Relish with skewered grilled swordfish
or spooned on avocado quarters

Pineapple Salsa with skewered grilled chicken or shrimp,
papaya wedges and nectarine slices

Greek Wedding Shower

SERVES 8

From the land of Aphrodite, the goddess of love, comes a menu to shower the guest of honor with distinctive flavors along with good wishes. All of the recipes can be made in advance and should be doubled to serve a celebration of 8. For no-fuss side dishes in the Greek theme, also serve a plate of dolmas (purchased at a delicatessen or specialty-food market) and a bowl of imported olives. Offer red and white wine, mineral water and iced tea—and let the toasts begin.

Greek Garlic Sauce with steamed asparagus spears

Greek Split Pea Purée with pita bread chips
and lavash crackers

Taramasalata with toast triangles and lemon wedges

Pomegranate and Walnut Paste with skewered grilled
chicken and fresh pear and apple slices

A Champagne Celebration

SERVES 6

When a special occasion calls for champagne, consider this elegant repast as a fitting accompaniment. Pull out your silver platters and crystal bowls, white linen cocktail napkins and traditional flutes. As a nonalcoholic yet sophisticated alternative to champagne, offer sparkling herbal beverages in pale golds and pinks, sold bottled like wine. Small porcelain hors d'oeuvre plates allow guests to assemble a collection of starters to nibble through pleasant conversations to come.

Eggplant Caviar with pita bread chips or
fresh pretzel bread sticks

Herbed Cheese Spread on crackers, slices of chewy
Italian bread, celery stalks and cucumber spears

Seafood Spread on toasted baguette slices

Tuscan Mushroom and Liver Spread using sliced cold
polenta for the bases, brushed with olive oil and
placed under the broiler for 2 minutes or until golden

DIPS

Dips are comfortable, unfussy and very convivial. They can transform even a formal occasion into a friendly shared activity and can literally bring a party together: Arms reach in concert to swirl carrot sticks or triangles of crispy chips in the communal bowl. Conversation flows as fellow nibblers try to guess the intertwining of flavors that gives so simple a food such delectable complexity.

For the host, dips are perhaps the easiest of appetizers. Preparation is usually minimal, although some tasks are done in stages and need to be planned accordingly. Most dips can be assembled ahead, completely or in part, ready to set out the moment the guests walk in the door or the instant the picnic blanket is unfurled.

Very portable, dips take a party anywhere and everywhere, indoors and out—to a lawn concert, to a lunch in the woods or on the dock, into the summer garden at its floriferous peak or to a movable feast passed back and forth in front of the television.

In this chapter you will find classics and exciting new tastes. They range from a seasoned olive oil dip for crisp raw vegetables to a fiery Thai chili paste that a frosty brew would cool down nicely. Remember, no utensils are required —that's part of the appeal. Simply offer bountiful accompaniments so everyone can dig right in.

Vegetables Dipped in Oil (recipe page 45)

25

large pinch of salt

6–12 cloves garlic

large pinch of fresh bread crumbs

2 egg yolks

2 cups (16 fl oz/500 ml) extra-
virgin olive oil

1¹/₂ tablespoons fresh lemon juice
or 1 teaspoon water

❶ AÏOLI

This garlic-infused mayonnaise from Provence conjures images of ancient olive groves, radiant sunshine and heady flavors. Paired with fresh vegetables, Aïoli is an almost effortless hors d'oeuvre that is easily expanded into a supper platter with leftover cold chicken or lamb or quickly poached fish and shellfish. It also improves any sandwich.

In a food processor fitted with the metal blade or in a blender, process the salt and 6 of the garlic cloves to form a paste. Add the remaining garlic cloves as desired. Add the bread crumbs and process into a consistent paste. Add the egg yolks and process the mixture until smooth.

With the motor running, pour in the olive oil in a slight trickle and gradually incorporate into the mixture. As the sauce begins to thicken noticeably, the oil may be poured in a steadier flow. The mixture should not become too stiff. After half of the oil has been incorporated, add the lemon juice or water. Continue adding oil and, if necessary, a bit of water until the desired quantity of sauce is reached. Transfer to a serving bowl. Aïoli can be kept in an airtight container in the refrigerator for 1–2 days.

MAKES ABOUT 2¹/₂ CUPS (20 FL OZ/625 ML); SERVES 6

BAGNA CAUDA

The Italians create an aromatic "bath" for vegetables and bread with just a few simple ingredients. (photograph page 73)

4 cloves garlic, minced

pinch of salt

³/₄ cup (6 fl oz/180 ml) extra-virgin olive oil

2 tablespoons unsalted butter

8–12 anchovy fillets, drained and chopped

In a small bowl, mash the garlic and salt with a fork to form a paste. Place the paste in a small, flameproof earthenware casserole or enameled ironware casserole over low heat. Add the olive oil, butter and 8 of the anchovy fillets and stir until all the ingredients melt together to form a sauce. Add the remaining anchovies, as desired, stirring until they melt into the sauce.

To serve, place the pan on a hot plate at low heat. Guests dip raw or blanched vegetables into the sauce and use a piece of bread to catch any drips when the vegetables are lifted from the dip. Bagna Cauda can be kept in an airtight container in the refrigerator for 2–3 days and reheated over low heat before serving.

MAKES 1 CUP (8 FL OZ/250 ML); SERVES 4

2 large avocados

1 tablespoon finely chopped onion

1 or 2 serrano chilies, sliced

1 large tomato, peeled and
   chopped

2 fresh cilantro (fresh coriander)
   sprigs, chopped

fresh lime juice

salt

❷ GUACAMOLE

A chunky texture is what you want here, so mash the avocados with a fork rather than purée them in a food processor or blender. If the avocados don't give to gentle finger pressure, ripen them further at room temperature in a paper bag for about 2 days. Serve Guacamole as a dip with tortilla chips, spoon it in tacos and burritos or use it as a brunch condiment alongside chili omelettes. (photograph pages 46–47)

Cut the avocados in half and remove the pits. Scoop out the flesh and place in a medium bowl. Mash with a fork.

Add the onion, chilies, tomato and cilantro and mix thoroughly. Add a few drops of lime juice and salt to taste. Transfer to a serving bowl. Although Guacamole is best served the day it is made, it can be stored in an airtight container in the refrigerator for 1 day. Add a few more drops of lime juice and stir before serving.

MAKES ABOUT 3 CUPS (24 FL OZ/750 ML); SERVES 6

2 tablespoons vegetable oil

2 cloves garlic, minced

1 large onion, finely chopped

2 cups (16 fl oz/500 ml)
refried beans

1¹/₂ cups (12 oz/375 g) grated
Manchego or Monterey Jack
cheese, plus more for sprinkling
if desired

¹/₄ cup (2 oz/65 g) diced, drained
canned jalapeño chilies or
2 tablespoons diced, seeded,
fresh jalapeño chilies

¹/₂ teaspoon ground cumin

salt and freshly ground pepper

PINTO BEAN DIP

With prepared refried beans and diced jalapeños in your pantry, this popular Southwestern dip can be assembled in minutes. Serve warm with tortilla chips. The diet-conscious can still indulge: substitute nonfat, vegetarian refried beans and baked pita chips. Manchego cheese is a rich, mellow cheese available in Latin markets and well-stocked supermarkets.

In a medium saucepan over medium heat, warm the oil and sauté the garlic and onions until soft, about 5 minutes. Add the beans, cheese, chilies and cumin and cook, stirring occasionally, over low heat until the cheese is melted and the beans are warmed through. Add salt and pepper to taste. Transfer to a chafing dish and sprinkle with additional grated cheese, if desired. The dip can be stored in an airtight container in the refrigerator for 2–3 days. Warm over low heat before serving.

MAKES ABOUT 4 CUPS (32 FL OZ/1 L); SERVES 8

*Top to bottom: Pinto Bean Dip,
Roasted Red Bell Pepper Dip (recipe page 32)*

ROASTED RED BELL PEPPER DIP

1 teaspoon extra-virgin olive oil

5 cloves garlic, peels intact

3 red bell peppers (capsicums), roasted, peeled and seeded

$1/2$ teaspoon ground cumin

4 oz (125 g) cream cheese at room temperature

2 tablespoons sour cream or crème fraîche

salt and freshly ground pepper

From one simple recipe evolve many options for entertaining. The rich blend of roasted garlic and red bell pepper brings out the best in any vegetable. You can also toss it with pasta as a quick first course or use it as a colorful topping for baked potatoes. To save time, roast the peppers and garlic ahead or buy prepared roasted peppers in a jar.

Preheat an oven to 350°F (180°C). Sprinkle the olive oil over the garlic cloves and wrap tightly in aluminum foil. Place in the oven until the cloves are soft, 40–60 minutes. Let cool.

Squeeze the soft garlic cloves from their peels into a blender or into a food processor fitted with the metal blade. Add the red peppers and cumin and purée. Add the cream cheese and blend until smooth. Transfer the mixture to a small bowl and fold in the sour cream or crème fraîche. Season to taste with salt and pepper. The dip can be stored in an airtight container in the refrigerator for 2–3 days.

MAKES ABOUT $1^1/2$ CUPS (12 FL OZ/375 ML); SERVES 4

1¹/₈ cups (¹/₂ lb/250 g) dried
   yellow split peas or dried
   fava (broad) beans

1 small onion, chopped

3 tablespoons extra-virgin olive oil

3¹/₂ cups (28 fl oz/875 ml) water

1 teaspoon salt, plus salt to taste

2 tablespoons chopped fresh dill
   (optional)

freshly ground pepper

FOR THE TOPPING:

2–4 tablespoons extra-virgin
   olive oil

2 tablespoons fresh lemon juice
   (optional)

chopped or thinly sliced red
   (Spanish) onion or green
   (spring) onions

freshly ground pepper

GREEK SPLIT PEA PURÉE

Soaked and simmered, dried split peas or fava beans collapse into a thick, delicious paste that simple seasonings transform into a luscious dip. Accompany the dip with pita bread triangles and cubes of salty feta cheese. The recipe must be made about 1 hour ahead, a boon for entertaining. (photograph page 35)

If using yellow split peas, rinse well under cold running water. If using fava beans, place in a bowl with water to cover generously and refrigerate overnight. To prepare the fava beans the same day, place the beans and 4 cups (32 fl oz/1 l) water in a medium saucepan, bring to a boil, simmer 15–20 minutes, remove from the heat and let stand 1 hour. Drain and rinse the refrigerated or simmered beans well under cold running water.

In a medium saucepan, combine the peas or beans, onion, oil, water and 1 teaspoon salt. Bring to a boil, reduce the heat to low, cover and simmer until the peas or beans are so soft that they have disintegrated, about 1 hour.

Transfer the peas or beans and their liquid to a food processor fitted with the metal blade and purée. Mix in the dill, if using, and salt and pepper to taste. Transfer the purée to a serving dish, cover with plastic wrap and allow to cool and thicken.

To serve, drizzle with the olive oil and the lemon juice, if using. Top with the onion and a grinding of pepper. The purée can be stored in an airtight container in the refrigerator for 2–3 days.

MAKES 3¹/₂ CUPS (28 FL OZ/875 ML); SERVES 4–6

TARAMASALATA

5 slices white bread, crusts discarded

¹/₂ cup (5 fl oz/155 ml) mullet roe (*tarama*)

1 onion, coarsely chopped

1 cup (8 fl oz/250 ml) extra-virgin olive oil

¹/₂ cup (4 fl oz/125 ml) fresh lemon juice

2 tablespoons chopped fresh flat-leaf (Italian) parsley or a small handful of imported black olives

Mullet roe is the only exotic ingredient in this speedy hors d'oeuvre that you prepare ahead and chill. It's available in bulk or by the jar at Middle Eastern markets. You can also use carp or cod roe. Pass a basket of warm, crusty bread for dunking, along with pencil-thin trimmed green onions, cucumber slices or spears, bright red radishes and celery fingers.

In a shallow bowl, combine the bread with just enough water to cover and let soak briefly. Remove the bread, squeeze dry and place in a food processor fitted with the metal blade or in a blender.

Add the roe and onion and process to mix. With the motor running, slowly add the oil and lemon juice, processing until a smooth paste forms. Transfer to a serving bowl. Cover and chill.

Serve chilled, garnished with the parsley or black olives. Taramasalata can be stored in an airtight container in the refrigerator for 2–3 days.

MAKES ABOUT 2¹/₂ CUPS (20 FL OZ/625 ML); SERVES 4–6

Left to right: Taramasalata,
Greek Split Pea Purée (recipe page 33)

Top to bottom: Sesame-Eggplant Purée, Hummus (recipe page 38)

2 globe eggplants (aubergines)

2 cloves garlic, very finely minced

$^1/_4$ cup (2$^1/_2$ oz/75 g) tahini

$^1/_3$–$^1/_2$ cup (3–4 fl oz/80–125 ml) fresh lemon juice, or to taste

salt and freshly ground pepper

3 tablespoons pine nuts, toasted

3 tablespoons chopped fresh flat-leaf (Italian) parsley

1 teaspoon ground cumin *(optional)*

2 tablespoons pomegranate seeds *(optional)*

❧ SESAME-EGGPLANT PURÉE

When pomegranates are plentiful in the fall, mine their jewellike crimson seeds for a seasonal garnish. To remove the seeds: Trim the blossom end, slash the rind in a few places, then soak the fruit in cold water for 5 minutes. Break the fruit apart under water and pluck out the seeds. Drain them and pat dry with paper towels. You can find tahini—sesame seed paste—at Middle Eastern shops, well-stocked markets and health-food stores.

Preheat a broiler (griller).

Place the eggplants on a baking sheet and slip under the broiler. Broil (grill), turning often, until charred on all sides and quite tender, 20–30 minutes. Remove from the broiler and let cool.

Cut the eggplants in half and scoop the pulp from the skins into a medium bowl or into a food processor fitted with the metal blade. Mash with a fork or pulse to purée.

Add the garlic, tahini and lemon juice and beat with a fork or process to purée. Season to taste with salt and pepper.

Transfer to a plate or shallow bowl. Sprinkle with the pine nuts and parsley, and with the cumin and pomegranate seeds, if using. The purée can be stored in an airtight container in the refrigerator for 2–3 days.

MAKES ABOUT 4 CUPS (32 FL OZ/1 L); SERVES 6–8

HUMMUS

Dried chick-peas are more authentic in this classic Middle Eastern dip, but using canned chick-peas is quicker. For the 1 cup dried chick-peas in this recipe, substitute 3 cups (1¼ lb/125 g) drained canned chick-peas. Tahini looks like peanut butter, but is made from ground sesame seeds. You'll find it in better supermarkets and specialty grocers. It may need a quick stirring before each use, as it can separate.

1 cup (7 oz/220 g) dried chick-peas (garbanzo beans)

4 cups (32 fl oz/1 l) water

¼ cup (2½ oz/75 g) tahini

2 cloves garlic, finely minced

¼ cup (2 fl oz/60 ml) fresh lemon juice, or to taste

salt

pinch of cayenne pepper

FOR THE TOPPING:
2 tablespoons extra-virgin olive oil

3 tablespoons chopped fresh flat-leaf (Italian) parsley

1 teaspoon ground cumin *(optional)*

½ teaspoon cayenne pepper *(optional)*

3 tablespoons pomegranate seeds *(optional; see note, page 37)*

Place the chick-peas in a medium bowl with water to cover generously; refrigerate overnight. To prepare the chick-peas the same day, place in a medium saucepan with water to cover generously, bring to a boil, simmer 2–3 minutes, remove from the heat and let stand 1 hour.

Drain the refrigerated or simmered chick-peas and rinse well under cold running water. Place in a medium saucepan, add the 4 cups (32 fl oz/1 l) water and bring to a boil. Reduce the heat to low, cover and simmer until very soft, 1 hour or longer.

Drain the chick-peas, reserving any liquid, and transfer to a food processor fitted with the metal blade. Pulse to purée. Add the tahini, garlic and lemon juice and purée. Add just enough reserved cooking liquid or enough cold water to achieve a spreadable consistency. Season with salt to taste and the cayenne.

If serving the purée immediately, spoon onto a shallow plate and smooth the top with a spoon or spatula. Drizzle with the olive oil and strew with the parsley. If desired, sprinkle on the cumin and cayenne and arrange the pomegranate seeds in a star pattern. Or the purée can be transferred to a bowl, covered and kept at room temperature for up to 6 hours or in the refrigerator for 1–2 days. Return to room temperature before serving. The mixture will thicken upon standing; thin with water or reserved cooking liquid.

MAKES ABOUT 3 CUPS (24 FL OZ/750 ML); SERVES 6–8

SPICY SHRIMP SAUCE

8 green Thai chilies (*prik khee noo*)

6 cloves garlic

2 tablespoons shrimp paste (*gapi*)

¹/₄ cup (2 fl oz/60 ml) fish sauce
   (*nam pla*)

¹/₃ cup (3 fl oz/90 ml) fresh
   lime juice

3 tablespoons palm sugar
   (*nam taan peep*)

10 whole large dried shrimp
   (prawns), rinsed in warm water

This fiery dip for fresh vegetables will please the many fans of Thai cuisine. It may require a trip to an Asian market, but if you like these flavors or entertain others who do, you can stock up on the essentials so you can prepare the dip a number of times without extra shopping.

Place the chilies, garlic cloves and shrimp paste in a blender or in a food processor fitted with the metal blade. Process until the garlic is crushed and combined with the other ingredients. Add the fish sauce, lime juice and palm sugar and process briefly to combine with the shrimp paste mixture. Add the dried shrimp and process to incorporate into the dip.

Transfer the dip to a serving bowl and allow the shrimp to soak in the sauce for about 15 minutes before serving. The dip can be stored in an airtight container in the refrigerator for 1–2 days.

MAKES ABOUT 1¹/₂ CUPS (12 FL OZ/375 ML); SERVES 4

THAI DIPPING SAUCE

½ cup (1 oz/30 g) dried shrimp (prawns)

4–6 long, slender eggplants (aubergines)

¼ cup (2 fl oz/60 ml) fish sauce (*nam pla*)

¼ cup (2 fl oz/60 ml) fresh lime juice

2 tablespoons sugar

Neutral-flavored eggplant is the perfect foil for salty fish sauce, a staple of Thai cooking and available at Asian markets and well-stocked supermarkets. Spinach and chard make attractive edible scoops for the chunky mixture, along with slices of cucumber and baby eggplant.

In a small bowl, soak the shrimp in warm water to cover for 10 minutes. Drain and set aside.

Place the eggplants in a medium saucepan and add water to cover. Bring to a boil, reduce the heat to low and cook until the eggplants are just soft and tender, 15–20 minutes.

Drain the eggplants, rinse in cold water until cool enough to handle and peel the skin. Roughly dice the eggplants.

Place the eggplant, shrimp, fish sauce, lime juice and sugar in a blender or in a food processor fitted with the metal blade. Process just until all ingredients are combined and form a coarse paste. Transfer to a serving bowl. The dip can be stored in a covered container in the refrigerator for 2–3 days.

MAKES ABOUT 2½ CUPS (20 FL OZ/625 ML); SERVES 4

1 fennel bulb

2 carrots

2 Belgian endives (witloof/ chicory)

1 cup (8 fl oz/240 ml) extra-virgin olive oil

salt and freshly ground pepper

VEGETABLES DIPPED IN OIL

The simplest of recipes results in a superb sauce if the olive oil is the finest and the vegetables bright and fresh. No party food is easier. In addition to fennel, carrots and Belgian endive, consider cauliflower, artichokes and radishes. You can also try this presentation with a favorite flavored olive oil.

Trim the base of the fennel bulb and cut the bulb into 6 wedges. Peel the carrots and cut them into slender sticks. Trim the Belgian endives and separate the leaves.

Arrange the vegetables on a serving dish. Divide the oil among 6 little bowls. Season each portion with salt and pepper.

Place the dish of vegetables in the center of the table and pass the bowls of oil.

MAKES 1 CUP (8 FL OZ/250 ML); SERVES 6

SALSAS

Classic salsas are variations of a theme—tomatoes or tart green tomatillos, onions, garlic and, of course, chilies from mild to incendiary. Roughly chopped and quickly tossed together, these few ingredients sing with freshness and flavor. You'll find such traditional renditions in this chapter to scoop with crunchy chips, tuck into quesadillas or dollop on tacos and burritos.

Mingled among these classics to intrigue your palate are the creative variations and unexpected twists that make today's salsas so exciting. Some updates are as simple as a touch of Asian rice vinegar for its extra tang and sweetness, or the addition of crunchy romaine lettuce for its clean, fresh flavor. Others are more dramatic. What about a spicy-sweet counterpoint of juicy pineapple and succulent papaya flamed with two kinds of chilies? Or a Mediterranean-inspired combination of ripe tomatoes, lemon and pine nuts?

Salsas can do much more than wake up your entertaining as a party opener. A spoonful transforms simple grilled or broiled fish, meat or poultry into a memorable main course. For a light lunch or supper, toss salsa with pasta, heap it on burgers or cascade it over fresh corn bread. For such a big return, salsa demands very little effort or time. And since salsas must sit several hours to marry the flavors, there's nothing last-minute to fuss with.

Top to bottom: Guacamole (recipe page 29), Tomato Salsa (recipe page 50), accompanied by taco sauce (right)

1/4 cup (1 1/2 oz/45 g) chopped nopalitos

4 New Mexico green or Anaheim chilies, roasted, peeled, seeded and diced

1 poblano chili, roasted, peeled, seeded and diced

1 green bell pepper (capsicum), seeded and diced

1 red or yellow bell pepper (capsicum), seeded and diced

1 serrano chili, seeded and diced

1/4 cup (1 oz/30 g) chopped red (Spanish) onion

1/2 cup (3 oz/90 g) chopped, husked tomatillos

1/2 cup (3 oz/90 g) chopped tomato

2 tablespoons fresh lime juice

1 tablespoon chopped fresh cilantro (fresh coriander)

salt

GREEN CHILI SALSA

Slightly tart, this salsa pairs well with grilled fish or poultry, quesadillas and tortilla chips. Nopalitos are julienned prickly pear cactus pads sold pickled at Latin grocery stores and specialty-food markets. Often mistaken for a green tomato, the citrusy tomatillo is another vegetable altogether and is identified by its papery husk. Most markets stock them.

Combine all the ingredients, including salt to taste, in a small bowl. Let stand at room temperature for 30 minutes before serving to allow the flavors to blend. The salsa can be kept, covered in the refrigerator, up to 1 week.

MAKES ABOUT 2 CUPS (16 FL OZ/500 ML); SERVES 4

4 or 5 tomatoes

1 large, firm cucumber

1 white onion

2 cloves garlic, minced

$^3/_4$ cup (1 oz/30 g) chopped fresh
   cilantro (fresh coriander)

3 tablespoons fresh lime juice

$^1/_4$ cup (2 fl oz/60 ml) seasoned
   rice vinegar

1 teaspoon ground cumin

2 large red bell peppers (capsicums)
   or 3 Anaheim chilies, roasted,
   peeled, seeded and chopped

salt and freshly ground pepper

TOMATO SALSA

Make this bright red, fresh salsa the hit of late-summer gatherings by using the best tomatoes from your garden or a crop fresh-picked at a farmer's market. Mild-flavored rice vinegar is borrowed from Japanese and Chinese sauces. It imparts an unexpected sweetness that is subtle and very pleasing. Serve this salsa as a starter or as a condiment on an omelette or on grilled fish or chicken.

Cut the tomatoes in half. Remove the seeds and excess juice. Chop the tomatoes. Peel and chop the cucumber and onion. In a large bowl, combine the tomatoes, cucumber and onion. Add the garlic and stir in the cilantro, lime juice, vinegar, cumin and peppers or chilies. Season to taste with salt and pepper. Chill before serving. The salsa can be kept in a covered container in the refrigerator for up to 1 week.

MAKES 4 CUPS (32 FL OZ/1 L); SERVES 8

6 plum (Roma) tomatoes,
   quartered, seeded and diced

$^1/_2$ teaspoon chopped fresh mint

$^1/_2$ teaspoon chopped fresh parsley

$^1/_2$ teaspoon fresh lemon juice

1 tablespoon extra-virgin olive oil

$^1/_4$ teaspoon grated lemon zest

$^1/_2$ teaspoon salt

$^1/_2$ teaspoon freshly ground pepper

$^1/_4$ cup ($1^1/_2$ oz/45 g) pine nuts,
   lightly toasted

TOMATO-MINT RELISH

Fresh, clean summery tastes brighten a condiment that hints of the Mediterranean. Spoon it across grilled or broiled tuna steaks and finish the plate with couscous and steamed asparagus for a winning company menu.

In a small bowl, combine all the ingredients, except the pine nuts. Let stand at room temperature for 1–2 hours to blend the flavors. Stir in the pine nuts just before serving. The relish can be stored in a covered container in the refrigerator for up to 1 week.

MAKES ABOUT 1$^1/_2$ CUPS (12 FL OZ/375 ML); SERVES 4

2 jalapeño chilies, seeded
and minced

1 bunch radishes, trimmed
and diced

1 cucumber, peeled, seeded
and diced

5 green (spring) onions, including
tender green tops, minced

5 tomatoes, diced

1 cup (6 oz/185 g) yellow cherry
tomatoes, halved

1/4 cup (1/3 oz/10 g) minced fresh
cilantro (fresh coriander) leaves

1/4 cup (2 fl oz/60 ml) extra-virgin
olive oil

3 tablespoons fresh lime juice or
balsamic vinegar

salt

GAZPACHO SALSA

When the weather gets balmy, grills fire up and so does outdoor socializing. Easy meals rule. The ingredients of a crunchy summer soup take new form as a chunky accompaniment for grilled meats that assembles quickly. It can also be spooned over grilled fingers of polenta or grits.

Combine all the ingredients, including salt to taste, in a medium bowl and stir well. Let stand at room temperature for 30 minutes before serving to allow the flavors to blend. The salsa can be kept in a covered container in the refrigerator for up to 1 week.

MAKES ABOUT 3 CUPS (24 FL OZ/750 ML); SERVES 8–10

Clockwise from top: Tomatillo Salsa, Pineapple Salsa (recipe page 56), Pumpkin Seed Salsa (recipe page 57)

4–6 tomatillos, husked and diced

2 Anaheim chilies, roasted, peeled, seeded and diced

1 red bell pepper (capsicum), roasted, peeled, seeded and diced

2 plum (Roma) tomatoes, diced

1 jalapeño chili, seeded and diced

$^{1}/_{2}$ cup ($1^{1}/_{2}$ oz/45 g) finely chopped green (spring) onions

2 cloves garlic, minced

1 teaspoon cumin seed, crushed to a coarse powder

2 tablespoons cider vinegar

1 tablespoon apple juice

salt and freshly ground pepper

TOMATILLO SALSA

Not tomatoes, although they resemble them, tomatillos taste like a combination of lemons and apples. They are sold with their papery tan husks still intact. This lovely green-and-red salsa enhances tortilla chips, cheese quesadillas and grilled fish, poultry or meat, served at any casual occasion.

Combine all the ingredients, including salt and pepper to taste, in a small bowl. Let stand at room temperature 1 hour before serving to allow the flavors to blend. The salsa can be kept in a covered container in the refrigerator for up to 1 week.

MAKES ABOUT $2^{1}/_{2}$ CUPS (20 FL OZ/625 ML); SERVES 4

1 large pineapple, peeled, cored
and diced

1 red bell pepper (capsicum),
seeded and diced

$1/2$ green bell pepper (capsicum),
seeded and diced

1 large red (Spanish) onion,
finely chopped

3 tablespoons minced fresh
cilantro (fresh coriander)

1 papaya, peeled, seeded and diced

2 tablespoons fresh lime juice

$1^1/_2$ teaspoons seasoned rice
vinegar

3 green (spring) onions, finely
chopped

1 habanero chili, finely chopped

$1/_8$ teaspoon cayenne pepper

salt and freshly ground pepper

PINEAPPLE SALSA

The spicy-sweet, hot taste of the tropics wakes up blue-corn tortilla chips, grilled fresh tuna or sautéed chicken. The habanero chili is incendiary, the world's most explosively hot chili, in fact, so be careful when handling it and use sparingly.

Combine all the ingredients, including salt and pepper to taste, in a medium bowl. Refrigerate until ready to serve. This salsa is best the day it is made, but will keep up to 1 week in a covered container in the refrigerator.

MAKES ABOUT 4 CUPS (32 FL OZ/1 L); SERVES 8

1 cup (6 oz/185 g) cooked
corn kernels

1 1/2 cups (9 oz/280 g) chopped
tomatoes

1 New Mexico green or Anaheim
chili, roasted, peeled, seeded
and chopped

1 red serrano chili, seeded and
diced

2 tablespoons fresh lime juice

1/4 teaspoon ground cumin

1 cup (5 oz/155 g) unsalted green
pumpkin seeds, toasted

salt and freshly ground pepper

PUMPKIN SEED SALSA

You can make this crunchy salsa with summer's sweet fresh corn. And with frozen kernels in your freezer, any seasonal limitations disappear. The delicate, crunchy, unsalted pumpkin seeds are called pepitas *in Latin markets. They are also available in well-stocked markets and health-food stores.*

In a medium bowl, combine all the ingredients, including salt and pepper to taste. The salsa can be stored in a covered container in the refrigerator for up to 1 week.

MAKES ABOUT 3 1/2 CUPS (28 FL OZ/875 ML); SERVES 6

kernels from 2 ears of raw or
   roasted corn

3 red bell peppers (capsicums),
   roasted, peeled, seeded and diced

$^1/_3$ cup (2 oz/60 g) cooked
   black beans

1 jalapeño chili, minced

1 red (Spanish) onion, chopped

$^1/_2$ cup ($^3/_4$ oz/20 g) chopped fresh
   cilantro (fresh coriander)

dash of sugar

juice of $^1/_2$ lime

dash of salt

 # PEPPER AND CORN SALSA

Top a Southwestern "pizza" with a confetti-colored salsa—stack whole wheat tortillas with cheese, tomatoes, shredded cooked chicken and sliced chilies, bake until bubbly, then add the salsa. Present with beer or wine, as a first course or light lunch or supper.

In a small bowl, combine all the ingredients, stirring to mix well. Set aside at room temperature 1 hour to allow the flavors to blend before serving. The salsa can be stored in an airtight container in the refrigerator for up to 1 week.

MAKES 2 CUPS (16 FL OZ/500 ML); SERVES 4

CHARRED GREEN SALSA

Roasting the vegetables gives this salsa a delicious smokiness, which is enhanced if you leave the blackened skin on the chilies. A whole head of romaine lettuce adds another shade of green, and its own fresh flavor, to the mixture.

6 poblano chilies, roasted, peeled (if desired) and seeded

1 lb (500 g) tomatillos, husks removed and roasted

1 large yellow onion

¹/₂ bunch fresh cilantro (fresh coriander)

1 head romaine (cos) lettuce

2–3 cloves garlic, chopped

4 cups (32 fl oz/1 l) chicken stock

salt

Roughly chop the chilies, tomatillos, onion, cilantro and lettuce. Place in a large saucepan. Add the garlic and chicken stock and place over medium heat. Bring to a fast simmer and cook until the liquid is reduced by about one-fourth, 10–15 minutes.

Remove from the heat, let cool briefly and transfer to a food processor fitted with the metal blade or to a blender. Process to purée. Season to taste with salt. Cool to room temperature before transferring to a serving bowl. The salsa can be stored in a covered container in the refrigerator for 2–3 days.

MAKES ABOUT 5 CUPS (40 FL OZ/1.25 L); SERVES 8–10

3/4 cup (4 oz/125 g) diced, peeled
mango

1/4 cup (3/4 oz/20 g) minced green
(spring) onions, including tender
green tops

1/4 cup (1 1/2 oz/45 g) diced red
bell pepper (capsicum)

1 jalapeño chili, seeded (if desired)
and minced

2 tablespoons minced fresh
cilantro (fresh coriander)

2 teaspoons chopped fresh basil

1 tablespoon fresh lime juice

1/2 teaspoon grated lime zest

1 tablespoon extra-virgin olive oil

1 small avocado, peeled, halved,
pitted and diced (optional)

 # MANGO SALSA

*A ripe mango exudes a tantalizing fragrance and yields slightly to gentle finger
pressure. This tropical fruit is a classic balance for spicy foods because it is cool,
soothing and sweet.*

In a small bowl, gently stir together all the ingredients. Cover and refrigerate
1 hour to allow the flavors to blend before serving. The salsa can be stored in
a covered container in the refrigerator for 3–4 days.

MAKES 2 CUPS (16 FL OZ/500 ML); SERVES 4–6

1 small papaya, peeled, seeded
and finely diced

1 red bell pepper (capsicum),
roasted, peeled, seeded and
finely diced

1 poblano chili, roasted, peeled,
seeded and finely diced

1 tablespoon fresh lime juice

2 tablespoons finely chopped fresh
cilantro (fresh coriander)

2 jalapeño chilies, seeded (if
desired) and minced

salt

PAPAYA-PEPPER RELISH

*Think fish as the main-course partner for this colorful hot-sweet condiment,
whether steaks or fillets, kabobs or even fish tacos. When lunch or dinner parties
move onto the deck or patio, a light, creamy soup topped with this fruity relish
is a refreshing start.*

In a small bowl, combine all the ingredients, including salt to taste, and stir
to combine. Cover and refrigerate until serving. The relish can be stored in a
covered container in the refrigerator for 3–4 days.

MAKES ABOUT 2 CUPS (16 FL OZ/500 ML); SERVES 4–6

2 tomatoes

1 small white onion, thickly sliced

1 serrano chili, halved and seeded

1 large red bell pepper (capsicum), halved and seeded

3 cloves garlic, minced

2 tablespoons fresh cilantro (fresh coriander) leaves

juice of $1/2$ lime

1 teaspoon ground cumin

ROASTED VEGETABLE SALSA

As a twist, all the vegetables are blackened under the broiler. The flavor is deep and delicious. Create an easy vegetarian feast with spinach-filled cornmeal crêpes and this splendid salsa.

Preheat a broiler (griller). Place the tomatoes, onion slices, chili halves and bell pepper halves on a baking sheet and slip under the broiler. Broil (grill) until blackened and blistered, turning as needed. The timing will depend upon distance from the heat source. Remove from the broiler and slip the bell pepper and chili halves into a paper bag and let stand until cool enough to handle. Then, using your fingertips or a small knife, peel off the skins. Core the tomatoes.

Place the bell peppers and chilies, tomatoes and onions in a food processor fitted with the metal blade or in a blender. Add the garlic, cilantro, lime juice and cumin and process until smooth. Transfer to a serving bowl. The salsa can be stored in a covered container in the refrigerator for up to 1 week.

MAKES ABOUT 1 $1/2$ CUPS (12 FL OZ/375 ML); SERVES 4

SPREADS

Artisan bakeries in many cities offer old-world rustic breads with good, honest flavors and the best ingredients. Nothing improves a good piece of bread like a special something to slather across it. To build on such a tasty foundation are spreads creamy smooth or pleasingly chunky, vegetable based or flavored with seafood or meat, mildly herbal or strongly garlicky. The pages ahead contain many to choose from, with international flavors that take a party on a world tour. Many spreads do double or even triple duty—as an hors d'oeuvre, in a supporting role to a main-course roast or sandwich, or as a pick-me-up when the afternoon drifts on and dinner is still hours away.

Regardless of texture, form or flavor, spreads are among the most popular starters. Few presentations are as inviting. A whirl of herbed cheese or a mound of vegetable nuggets beckons sampling on toasted baguette slices or crispy crackers. The message is "help yourself." Even the host can relax, as most of the work takes place hours before guests arrive.

Thanks to a food processor or blender, even complex mixtures of vegetables, nuts and seeds emerge almost instantly as velvety smooth purées. A mortar and pestle is a less costly alternative in many cases to these electric appliances and, for some of the recipes, the more authentic tool. With any of these able assistants, your spreads will move quickly from kitchen to table.

Herbed Cheese Spread (recipe page 83)

4 whole heads garlic

salt and freshly ground pepper

$^1/_4$ cup (2 fl oz/60 ml) extra-virgin
  olive oil

ROASTED WHOLE GARLIC

Pugnacious raw garlic emerges from roasting as subdued, sweet and soft as butter, something new and wonderful. Squeeze individual cloves and spread the paste on toasted baguette slices or swirl into soups, sauces or mashed potatoes.

Preheat an oven to 225°F (110°C).

With a small, sharp knife, make an incision around the middle of each head of garlic, piercing the skin without cutting through the cloves. Peel the outer layer of papery skin from the top half of the head only, exposing the tops of the cloves. Place the heads of garlic in a baking dish, sprinkle generously with salt and pepper and drizzle with the olive oil.

Bake for about 20 minutes, then cover the baking dish with aluminum foil and continue baking, basting occasionally with the oil in the pan, until the garlic is very soft when squeezed, about 1 hour. Serve while still warm.

SERVES 6–8

❦ CHARRED ONION AND GARLIC SPREAD

1 whole head garlic

extra-virgin olive oil, as needed

1 onion, cut into slices $1/2$ in (12 mm) thick

$1/2$ lb (250 g) cream cheese or Neufchâtel cheese, at room temperature

salt and freshly ground pepper

2 green (spring) onions, including tender green tops, minced

2 tablespoons minced fresh flat-leaf (Italian) parsley

1 teaspoon Cajun-style seasoning

salted, roasted pumpkin seeds or toasted pine nuts for garnish

Two savory relatives, onion and garlic, star in a heady spread to slather on crackers or slices of crusty baguette. To continue the theme, use a hollowed onion as the serving container. A dollop of this spread on a baked potato or tossed with angel-hair pasta is memorable.

Separate the garlic cloves and peel them. Place the garlic cloves in a small saucepan and add olive oil to cover. Place over low heat and bring to a simmer. Cook until the cloves are softened but not browned, about 10 minutes. Remove from the heat and set aside.

Place a heavy frying pan or cast-iron griddle over medium-high heat. Add the onion slices in a single layer. Press down on them, turning when they begin to caramelize and char, after about 15 minutes. Repeat the process on the second side. Remove from the heat and set aside.

Drain the garlic cloves. Engage the motor in a food processor fitted with the metal blade and drop the garlic cloves down the feed tube. When the garlic is puréed, add the onion slices and pulse to combine. Add the cream cheese or Neufchâtel cheese, salt and pepper to taste, green onions, parsley and Cajun-style seasoning. Process until smooth.

Transfer the spread to a serving bowl, garnish with the pumpkin seeds or pine nuts, and serve at room temperature. The spread can be stored in a covered container in the refrigerator for 3–4 days.

MAKES ABOUT $1 1/2$ CUPS (12 FL OZ/375 ML); SERVES 4

3/4 cup (6 fl oz/180 ml) extra-
virgin olive oil

1 teaspoon herb vinegar

6–8 anchovy fillets, drained

freshly ground pepper

1 day-old baguette, cut crosswise
into quarters or eighths, then
split in half lengthwise and dried
in a low oven

3–4 cloves garlic

ANCHOVY SPREAD WITH GARLIC

A magnificent flavor evolves as the dried bread soaks up salty anchovies smoothed with olive oil and punctuated with garlic. Slathering the spread on bread, then grilling it, sets the mixture and gives it depth.

Prepare a fire in a charcoal grill or preheat a broiler (griller).

Warm the olive oil, vinegar and 6 of the anchovy fillets in a flameproof earthenware casserole or heavy sauté pan over the lowest possible heat. The anchovies should not cook, but will melt in contact with the heat. Add pepper to taste and stir to mix. Add the remaining anchovies, as desired, stirring until they melt into the oil.

Rub the dried cut surfaces of the bread with the garlic cloves and brush with the oil-anchovy mixture. Set aside until the bread is thoroughly saturated, about 1 hour.

Place the bread slices, crust side down, on the grill rack over the dying embers or under the broiler. Turn and grill on the anchovy spread side. Serve while still hot. The spread can be made a day in advance, stored in a covered container in the refrigerator and warmed before using.

SERVES 6–8

*Top to bottom: Bagna Cauda (recipe page 28),
Anchovy Spread with Garlic*

1 tablespoon ground dried
red chili

1 teaspoon ground cumin

1^1/$_2$ cups (6 oz/185 g) walnuts,
toasted

^{1}/$_2$ cup (2 oz/60 g) fine dried
bread crumbs

^{1}/$_4$ cup (2 fl oz/60 ml) extra-virgin
olive oil

2 tablespoons pomegranate syrup

pinch of sugar

salt

chopped fresh flat-leaf (Italian)
parsley for garnish

❼ POMEGRANATE AND WALNUT PASTE

Walnuts and dried bread crumbs add meaty texture to a spread for pita bread, cooked meats or fish. For additional texture and color, add two roasted, peeled and seeded red bell peppers to the purée, along with ^{1}/$_4$ cup (2 fl oz/60 ml) tomato purée. Sweet-tart pomegranate syrup is more concentrated than pomegranate juice. Look for it in Middle Eastern markets or substitute lemon juice.

In a food processor fitted with the metal blade or in a blender, combine the ground chili, cumin, walnuts, bread crumbs, olive oil, pomegranate syrup, sugar and salt to taste. Purée until smooth.

Transfer to a serving bowl. Chill until ready to serve, then garnish with the parsley. The paste can be stored in a covered container in the refrigerator for 2–3 days.

MAKES ABOUT 2 CUPS (16 FL OZ/500 ML); SERVES 4

3 long, slender eggplants
  (aubergines)

2 cloves garlic, minced

2–4 anchovy fillets, drained

4–5 tablespoons (2–3 fl oz/60–90
  ml) extra-virgin olive oil

salt and freshly ground pepper

EGGPLANT CAVIAR

From France's golden corner—Provence—comes a warm, garlicky spread for crusty grilled bread. Accompanied by a chilled white or rosé wine, it makes a complete appetizer.

Preheat an oven to 350°F (180°C).

Prick the eggplants several times and place in a shallow baking dish. Bake until the flesh is very soft when pierced with the tip of a knife, about 45 minutes. Remove the eggplants from the oven and, when cool enough to handle, split them in half. Using a spoon, scrape the flesh into a food processor fitted with the metal blade or into a blender. Process to purée.

Add the garlic and anchovies to taste and process to combine. With the motor running, slowly pour in the olive oil and process until the mixture has a spreadable consistency. Season to taste with salt and pepper. Eggplant Caviar can be stored in an airtight container in the refrigerator for 2–3 days.

MAKES ABOUT 2 CUPS (16 FL OZ/500 ML); SERVES 4

*Clockwise from top: Tuna Pâté (recipe page 78), Tuscan Mushroom and Liver Spread,
Seafood Spread (recipe page 79)*

TUSCAN MUSHROOM AND LIVER SPREAD

2 slices dried porcini mushrooms

6 oz (200 g) calf's liver

2 tablespoons extra-virgin olive oil

2 oz (60 g) pancetta, chopped

1/4 cup (2 fl oz/60 ml) dry red wine

1 plum (Roma) tomato, peeled
and chopped

1 teaspoon fennel seed

1 teaspoon juniper berries

salt

1 tablespoon unsalted butter,
at room temperature

Italians love to snack on toasted bread rounds with savory toppings, which they call crostini. This earthy mixture from Florence features calf's liver and meaty porcini mushrooms.

In a small bowl, soak the mushroom slices in warm water to cover for 30 minutes. Drain and squeeze out any excess moisture. Cut the liver into 2-in (5-cm) slices about 1/4 in (6 mm) thick.

In a medium sauté pan over high heat, warm the olive oil. Add the liver and pancetta and cook, stirring, until the liver changes color, about 5 minutes.

Add the wine, tomato, fennel seed, juniper berries, mushrooms and salt to taste. Reduce the heat to moderate and cook until the liquid evaporates, about 5 minutes.

Remove from the heat. Place the mixture in a food processor fitted with the metal blade and process until fairly smooth; be careful not to overprocess. Add the butter and blend in with a fork just until combined. Transfer to a serving bowl and serve while still warm. Although the spread is best the day it is made, it can be stored in a covered container in the refrigerator for 1 day.

MAKES ABOUT 1 1/2 CUPS (10 FL OZ/310 ML); SERVES 4–6

1 can (6 oz/180 g) tuna in olive oil, drained

$^1/_4$ cup (2 oz/60 g) unsalted butter, softened

1 tablespoon chopped fresh flat-leaf (Italian) parsley

1 tablespoon chopped onion

1 teaspoon fresh lemon juice

pinch of white pepper

TUNA PÂTÉ

This country appetizer is appealing for good reason: it's delicious, it's easy, and it goes together instantly with pantry foods. Nibble it on hot toast with a glass of cold white wine.

Flake the tuna and place it in a medium bowl. Add the butter, parsley, onion and lemon juice and, using a fork, mash into the tuna until thoroughly combined. Season with the pepper and mix well. Transfer to a serving bowl and refrigerate until serving. The pâté can be stored in the refrigerator in a covered container for 1 day.

MAKES 1$^1/_4$ CUPS (10 FL OZ/310 ML); SERVES 4–6

SEAFOOD SPREAD

Fresh shellfish makes an elegant canapé to serve warm, swirled on golden baguette toasts.

1 small squid or 6 sea scallops

6 mussels

6 clams

6 shrimp (prawns), heads removed

3 tablespoons extra-virgin olive oil

2 cloves garlic, chopped

pinch of ground dried chili

¹/₄ cup (2 fl oz/60 ml) dry white wine

1 plum (Roma) tomato, peeled and chopped

salt

1 tablespoon finely chopped fresh flat-leaf (Italian) parsley

Pull the tentacles from the squid body, if using. Discard the entrails, ink sac and cartilage from the body. Cut the tentacles off at the point just above the eyes and discard the head. Rinse the body and tentacles under cold running water. Set aside.

Remove the mussel and clam meats from their shells. Peel and devein the shrimp.

Heat the olive oil in a large sauté pan over moderate heat. Add the squid or scallops, mussels, clams, shrimp, garlic and chili and cook, stirring, for 2 minutes. Add the wine and tomato and season to taste with salt. Cook until the liquid evaporates, about 3 minutes. Remove from the heat.

Scoop the seafood mixture from the skillet onto a cutting surface. Chop the mixture fairly finely. Transfer to a serving bowl. Add the parsley and stir well. The spread can be stored in a covered container in the refrigerator for 6–8 hours and brought to room temperature before serving.

MAKES ABOUT 2 CUPS (16 FL OZ/500 ML); SERVES 6

SALT COD MOUSSE

After soaking for a day, salt cod whitens and doubles in bulk. Cooked until flaky, then whipped with milk, garlic and fruity olive oil, it becomes a soothing mousse that is a specialty of Provence. A bite on toasted bread brings to mind a sun-dappled terrace and lazy afternoons.

1¹/₂ lb (750 g) boneless dried salt cod

1¹/₂ cups (12 fl oz/375 ml) extra-virgin olive oil

1¹/₄ cups (10 fl oz/310 ml) milk

2 cloves garlic, puréed

juice of 1 lemon

freshly grated nutmeg

freshly ground pepper

Place the salt cod in a medium bowl and add water to cover. Refrigerate for 24–48 hours, changing the water at least 4 times. The amount of soaking necessary will depend upon the saltiness of the cod; thicker pieces may take longer than thinner pieces.

Drain the cod and place in a large saucepan with water to cover. Bring to a boil, cover, reduce the heat to low and poach gently until just tender, 8–10 minutes. Drain and cool slightly. Remove all traces of skin and any small bones and flake the cod with your fingers or a fork.

In a small saucepan over low heat, warm the oil. In another small saucepan over low heat, warm the milk. Place the flaked cod in a food processor fitted with the metal blade. Add the garlic and pulse once to combine. Add half of the warm oil, a bit at a time, processing to combine. Then slowly mix in half of the warm milk. Slowly beat in the remaining warm oil and then the remaining warm milk. Add only as much of the remaining oil, bit by bit, as is needed to achieve a very pale, thick and smooth mixture. Add the lemon juice and some nutmeg and season to taste with pepper.

Spoon onto a serving dish and serve while still warm. The mousse can be stored in a covered container in the refrigerator for 1 day and reheated in a double boiler over low heat.

MAKES ABOUT 3¹/₂ CUPS (28 FL OZ/875 ML); SERVES 6–8

Left to right: Tapénade (recipe page 82), Salt Cod Mousse

TAPÉNADE

1 cup (5 oz/155 g) Niçoise or oil-cured black olives, pitted

6 anchovy fillets, drained and chopped

2 tablespoons capers, rinsed and coarsely chopped

2 cloves garlic, finely chopped

juice of 1 lemon

4–6 tablespoons (2–3 fl oz/60–90 ml) extra-virgin olive oil

2 tablespoons Cognac (*optional*)

Totally pulled from the pantry, this savory olive spread is as useful as butter and keeps a week in the refrigerator. What could be better? Spoon it on warm bread, blend it with hard-cooked egg yolks for stuffed eggs or slip it under the skin of chicken before roasting or grilling.

In a food processor fitted with the metal blade or in a blender, combine the olives, anchovies, capers, garlic and lemon juice. Process to form a paste. With the motor running, slowly add enough of the oil to form a spoonable mixture. Stir in the Cognac, if using.

Transfer to a small serving bowl and serve at room temperature. Tapénade can be stored in a covered container in the refrigerator for up to 1 week.

MAKES ABOUT 2 CUPS (16 FL OZ/500 ML); SERVES 6

8 oz (250 g) ricotta cheese or
  fresh *fromage blanc*

1/4 cup (2 fl oz/60 ml) extra-virgin
  olive oil

3 tablespoons white wine vinegar

3 tablespoons dry white wine

3/4 cup (6 fl oz/200 ml) chilled
  cream

2 shallots, finely chopped

6 fresh flat-leaf (Italian) parsley
  sprigs, leaves only, finely chopped

6 fresh chervil sprigs, leaves only,
  finely chopped

10 fresh chive stalks, finely
  chopped

salt and freshly ground pepper

HERBED CHEESE SPREAD

The seasoned cheese that you buy can't compare with your own, especially if the herbs are snipped from a sunny windowsill garden. A dense, whole-grain country bread or chewy rye does the spread justice. (photograph pages 66–67)

Set the cheese to drain in a colander for 12 hours before preparing the recipe. Turn the drained cheese into a small bowl and mash with a fork. Mix in the oil, vinegar and wine.

In another small bowl, whip the cream until stiff. Fold into the cheese mixture. Mix in the shallots, parsley, chervil, chives and salt and pepper to taste. Place in a serving bowl and chill thoroughly before serving. The spread can be stored in a covered container in the refrigerator for 3–4 days.

MAKES ABOUT 2 CUPS (16 FL OZ/500 ML); SERVES 6

MADE WITH BREAD:

3 slices white bread, crusts discarded and bread crumbled (about $1/2$ cup/1 oz/30 g)

1 cup ($5^1/2$ oz/170 g) almonds, ground

4–6 cloves garlic, minced

salt

$1/4$ cup (2 fl oz/60 ml) red wine vinegar or 3 tablespoons fresh lemon juice

$3/4$–1 cup (6–8 fl oz/180–250 ml) extra-virgin olive oil

MADE WITH POTATOES:

1 lb (500 g) boiled or baked potatoes

4–6 cloves garlic, minced

salt

1 egg yolk (*optional*)

$1/4$ cup (2 fl oz/60 ml) red wine vinegar

$3/4$–1 cup (6–8 fl oz/180–250 ml) extra-virgin olive oil

❂ GREEK GARLIC SAUCE

From simple ingredients come some of the world's most delectable flavors and hospitable foods. The Greeks dress cooked beets, cauliflower, green beans and seafood with this pungent sauce. The version made with bread and almonds has a pleasing texture. Using potatoes results in a creamier consistency. Either version of the sauce can be stored in a covered container in the refrigerator for 1–2 days.

MADE WITH BREAD:

In a food processor fitted with the metal blade, purée the bread, almonds, garlic and salt to taste to form a paste. Mix in the vinegar or lemon juice. Gradually add the oil, a few drops at a time, and process until the mixture is thick and creamy. Add only as much oil as is needed to achieve the proper consistency. Transfer to a serving dish.

MADE WITH POTATOES:

Remove the skins from the potatoes. In a food processor fitted with the metal blade, purée the potatoes, garlic cloves and salt to taste. Add the egg yolk (if using) and the vinegar, processing to mix thoroughly. Gradually add the olive oil, a few drops at a time, and process until the mixture is thick and creamy. Add only as much oil as is needed to achieve the proper consistency. Transfer to a serving dish.

MAKES ABOUT $2^1/2$ CUPS (20 FL OZ/625 ML); SERVES 6

❼ BRIE WITH ROASTED GARLIC AND OLIVES

Garlic enhances everything, even an already perfect wheel of Brie. This combination is heavenly. Except for warming the cheese, all the preparation can be done ahead. As guests arrive, slip the wheels in the oven. For a barbecue, place the Brie in a shallow metal pan and set on a grill rack over a charcoal fire.

1 whole head garlic

1 fresh rosemary sprig

¹/₄ cup (2 fl oz/60 ml) extra-virgin olive oil

2 wheels (4 oz/125 g each) Brie cheese

¹/₄ cup (1 oz/40 g) sliced Kalamata olives

¹/₄ cup (2 oz/60 g) sliced dry-packed sun-dried tomatoes, reconstituted in water to cover, drained and cut into julienne strips

2 tablespoons pine nuts, lightly toasted

2 tablespoons minced fresh flat-leaf (Italian) parsley

2 tablespoons minced fresh basil

Preheat an oven to 375°F (190°C).

Remove any loose papery skin from the garlic head and place the garlic in a small baking dish. Add the rosemary sprig and olive oil, then cover tightly with aluminum foil. Bake until the garlic is soft when the cloves are pierced with a knife, about 35 minutes. Remove from the oven and let cool.

Raise the oven temperature to 400°F (200°C).

Using a sharp knife, slice the thin rind off the top of each Brie wheel. Place the wheels on an ovenproof serving plate. Press the garlic cloves free from their skins and spread the garlic evenly on the trimmed surface of each Brie wheel. Top with the olives, sun-dried tomatoes and pine nuts. Bake, uncovered, until the Brie is warm and softened, about 12 minutes.

Remove from the oven and sprinkle with the parsley and basil.

SERVES 8–10

1³/₄ cups (11 oz/345 g) red or
    yellow lentils

2 teaspoons salt, plus salt to taste

1 teaspoon turmeric

2 whole dried red chilies

4 cups (32 fl oz/1 l) water

1-in (2.5-cm) piece fresh ginger,
    peeled

3–4 cloves garlic

1 large onion, quartered

2 tablespoons *ghee* (clarified
    butter)

2 medium tomatoes, finely
    chopped

1¹/₂ teaspoons *garam masala* or a
    mild commercial curry powder

2–3 tablespoons cream *(optional)*

chili powder or chopped fresh
    cilantro (fresh coriander) or
    fresh mint

LENTIL PURÉE

A rich, smooth purée from India adds an exotic note to an hors d'oeuvres buffet or to a main course. Like curry powder, garam masala *is a blend of different spices.* Ghee *has a nuttier flavor than regular clarified butter because the milk solids are browned. Both are sold in well-stocked supermarkets or in Asian or Indian markets—*garam masala *in packages,* ghee *in bottles or tubs. Or use commercial curry powder and your own clarified butter (page 17).*

Wash the lentils thoroughly, drain and place in a medium saucepan with the 2 teaspoons salt and turmeric. Add the chilies and water, cover and bring to a boil. Reduce the heat and simmer until softened, about 12 minutes, skimming the surface occasionally to remove the froth and broken lentils.

In a food processor fitted with the metal blade or in a blender, finely chop the ginger, garlic and onion. In a medium sauté pan over medium heat, warm the *ghee.* Add the ginger-onion mixture and cook for 3–4 minutes. Add the tomatoes and *garam masala* or curry powder and cook for 2–3 minutes.

Drain the cooked lentils if excess liquid remains and return to their saucepan. Stir in the vegetable-curry mixture, season with salt to taste and simmer for 2–3 minutes. Add the cream, if using, and reheat the purée briefly. Transfer to a serving dish and sprinkle with the chili powder or garnish with the chopped fresh cilantro or mint. The purée can be kept in a covered container in the refrigerator for 4–5 days.

MAKES ABOUT 5 CUPS (40 FL OZ/1.25 L); SERVES 10–12

WHITE BEAN MOUSSE

6 cups (2^1/$_2$ lb/1.25 kg) cooked Great Northern beans

1 cup (8 fl oz/250 ml) extra-virgin olive oil

about ^{1}/$_2$ cup (4 fl oz/125 ml) milk, heated

freshly ground pepper

4–6 anchovy fillets, drained and chopped

juice of ^{1}/$_2$ lemon

salt

Serve as a starter or as a hearty accompaniment to roast lamb or pork. As a time-saver, substitute drained canned beans.

Purée the cooked beans in a food processor fitted with the metal blade and spoon them into a medium saucepan. Place the saucepan over very low heat. Beat the purée and gradually add the olive oil, a few drops at a time. Do not use all of the oil if the consistency of the purée is smooth. Beat in only enough of the milk for the purée to remain very smooth without being pourable. Season generously with pepper and stir in the anchovies and lemon juice. Add salt to taste.

Transfer the purée to a heated, deep serving platter. The mousse can be stored in an airtight container in the refrigerator for 1–2 days.

MAKES ABOUT 7 CUPS (56 FL OZ/1.75 L); SERVES 10–12

2 eggplants (aubergines)

salt

2 tablespoons plus 1¹/₂ cups
  (12 fl oz/375 ml) extra-virgin
  olive oil

1 cup (5 oz/155 g) diced celery

1 large red bell pepper (capsicum),
  seeded and cubed

1 large green bell pepper
  (capsicum), seeded and cubed

3 onions, chopped or sliced ¹/₄ in
  (6 mm) thick

1 cup (8 fl oz/250 ml) tomato
  purée

3 tablespoons capers, rinsed
  and drained

12 black and/or green olives,
  pitted and coarsely chopped

¹/₂ cup (4 fl oz/125 ml) red
  wine vinegar

2 tablespoons sugar

freshly ground pepper

CAPONATA

Don't be deterred by the many ingredients for this delectable Italian eggplant compote. When guests arrive, the work is long done, as the simple preparation can be completed a day ahead so the flavors can blend. Serve with toasted bread or as part of an antipasto assortment.

Peel the eggplants, if desired. Cut into 1-in (2.5-cm) dice. Sprinkle with salt and place in a colander for about 1 hour to drain. Rinse and pat dry.

In a small sauté pan over medium heat, warm the 2 tablespoons olive oil. Add the celery and bell peppers and sauté briefly; they should still be crisp. Set aside.

In a large sauté pan over medium-high heat, warm 1 cup (8 fl oz/250 ml) of the olive oil. Add the eggplant and sauté, turning often, until golden and cooked through, 15–20 minutes. Do not undercook. Using a slotted spoon, remove to paper towels to drain.

In the same sauté pan, warm the remaining ¹/₂ cup (4 fl oz/125 ml) olive oil over medium-high heat. Add the onions and sauté until tender and translucent, 8–10 minutes. Add the reserved celery and bell peppers and the tomato purée and simmer, stirring occasionally, for 10 minutes. Add the cooked eggplant, capers, olives, vinegar and sugar. Stir well and simmer, uncovered, over low heat for 20 minutes. Season to taste with salt and pepper.

Transfer to a serving bowl and serve at room temperature. Caponata can be stored in a covered container in the refrigerator for 4–5 days.

MAKES ABOUT 8 CUPS (64 FL OZ/2 L); SERVES 10–12

about 1 cup (8 fl oz/250 ml)
extra-virgin olive oil

8 onions, coarsely chopped

10 long, slender eggplants
(aubergines), cut into
large cubes

6 red, yellow and green bell
peppers (capsicums), seeded
and cut into squares

8 tomatoes, peeled, seeded and
coarsely chopped

1 head garlic, cloves separated
and peeled

handful of coarse sea salt

large bouquet garni, including
3 bay leaves and several fresh
thyme sprigs

6 small, firm zucchini (courgettes),
quartered length-wise and thickly
sliced crosswise

freshly ground pepper

fresh basil leaves

RATATOUILLE

*When summer's abundance is at its height, prepare this French bistro mélange
in quantity. It keeps for 4–5 days, getting even better as the flavors intermingle.*

Warm half of the olive oil in an 8–10-qt (8–10-l) stockpot over low heat.
Cook the onions until softened, about 10 minutes. Add the eggplants, bell
peppers, tomatoes and garlic cloves. Add the salt and stir gently, scraping the
bottom of the pot, until the vegetables release their liquid. Raise the heat to
medium, bring the liquid to a boil and simmer 20–30 minutes.

Bury the bouquet garni beneath the vegetables, reduce the heat to maintain a
light, bubbling simmer and cover with the lid slightly ajar. After about 30
minutes, add the zucchini, forcing it beneath the surface. Simmer until all of
the vegetables are meltingly tender, 45 minutes to 1 hour.

Place a large colander with a base inside a large, heavy sauté pan. Slowly and
carefully pour the contents of the stockpot into the colander. Let the vegetables drain for a couple of minutes, then prop the colander over the empty
stockpot to continue draining.

Place the pan with the juices over high heat, bring to a boil, then reduce the
heat to maintain a gentle boil. Place a platter beside the stockpot and, from
time to time, move the colander to the platter to empty newly drained juices
from the stockpot into the reducing liquid. About 1 hour is required for the
juices to reduce to a deep, mahogany-colored syrup with a foamy boil. To-
ward the end of the reduction, stir the juices often and remove the pan from
the heat when the foamy boil begins to subside into a staccato bubble.

Return the vegetables to the stockpot, remove the bouquet garni and pour in
the reduced juices. Gently stir the vegetables until they are evenly coated with
the reduced juices, then turn into a large dish to cool. Add pepper to taste and
stir in several spoonfuls of the remaining olive oil. Tear the basil leaves into
fragments and scatter over the top.

MAKES 2 1/2 QUARTS (80 FL OZ/2.5 L); SERVES 16–18

ACKNOWLEDGMENTS

Recipes and photographs in *Dips, Salsas & Spreads* first appeared in the following *Beautiful Cookbooks.*

RECIPES

Asia the Beautiful Cookbook, copyright © 1987, page 88. *California the Beautiful Cookbook,* copyright © 1991, page 68. *France the Beautiful Cookbook,* copyright © 1989, page 83. *Mediterranean the Beautiful Cookbook,* copyright © 1994, pages 33, 34, 37, 38, 74, 81, 82, 84, 90. *Mexico the Beautiful Cookbook,* copyright © 1991, page 29. *Pacific Northwest the Beautiful Cookbook,* copyright © 1993, page 50. *Provence the Beautiful Cookbook,* copyright © 1993, pages 27, 28, 73, 75, 89, 93. *Southwest the Beautiful Cookbook,* copyright © 1994, pages 31, 32, 49, 55, 56, 57. *Texas the Beautiful Cookbook,* copyright © 1995, pages 52, 53, 59, 60, 61, 63, 65, 71, 87. *Thailand the Beautiful Cookbook,* copyright © 1992, pages 41, 42. *Tuscany the Beautiful Cookbook,* copyright © 1992, pages 45, 77, 78, 79.

PHOTOGRAPHY

E. J. Armstrong, copyright © 1994, pages 2, 19, 30, 46–47, 48, 54, 58, 64; copyright © 1995, pages 1, 8, 13, 14, 60, 61, 62, 86. **John Callanan,** copyright © 1993, page 70. **Michael Freeman,** copyright © 1993, pages 28, 39. **John Hay,** copyright © 1992, pages 40, 43. **Pierre Hussenot,** copyright © 1989, pages 66–67. **Peter Johnson,** copyright © 1991, page 91; copyright © 1992, pages 24–25, 44, 76; copyright © 1993, pages 26, 72, 75, 92; copyright © 1994, pages 6–7, 35, 36, 74, 80, 85. **Allan Rosenberg,** copyright © 1991, pages 29, 51, 69.

INDEX